KYRIE

KYRIE

poems

Ellen Bryant Voigt

W · W · NORTON & COMPANY

NEW YORK • LONDON

The text of this book is composed in 11/15 Clearface Regular
with the display set in Clearface Bold
Composition by The Maple-Vail Manufacturing Group
Manufacturing by Courier Companies, Inc.
Book design by Jam Design

Library of Congress Cagaloging-in-Publication Data

Voigt, Ellen Bryant, 1943–
Kyrie / Ellen Bryant Voigt.
p.   cm.
I. Title.
PS3572.034K97   1995
811'.54—dc20   94-37900

ISBN 0-393-03796-7

W. W. Norton & Company, Inc., 500 Fifth Avenue, New York, N.Y. 10110
W. W. Norton & Company Ltd., 10 Coptic Street, London WC1A 1PU

1 2 3 4 5 6 7 8 9 0

for Dudley and Will

Nothing else—no infection, no war, no famine—
has ever killed so many in as short a period.

Alfred Crosby
America's Forgotten Pandemic:
The Influenza of 1918

KYRIE

PROLOGUE

After the first year, weeds and scrub;
after five, juniper and birch,
alders filling in among the briars;
ten more years, maples rise and thicken;
forty years, the birches crowded out,
a new world swarms on the floor of the hardwood forest.

And who can tell us where there was an orchard,
where a swing, where the smokehouse stood?

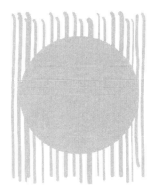

All ears, nose, tongue and gut,
dogs know if something's wrong;
chickens don't know a thing, their brains
are little more than optic nerve—
they think it's been a very short day
and settle in the pines, good night,
head under wing, near their cousins
but welded to a lower branch.

bird-brain

Dogs, all kinds of dogs—signals
are their job, they cock their heads,
their backs bristle, even house dogs
wake up and circle the wool rug.
Outside, the vacant yard: then,
within minutes something eats the sun.

nervous

eclispe

Dear John

〰

Dear Mattie, You're sweet to write me every day.
The train was not so bad, I found a seat,
watched the landscape flatten until dark,
ate the lunch you packed, your good chess pie.
I've made a friend, a Carolina man
who looks like Emmett Cocke, same big grin,
square teeth. Curses hard but he can shoot.
Sergeant calls him Pug I don't know why.
It's hot here but we're not here for long.
Most all we do is march and shine our boots.
In the drills they keep us 20 feet apart
on account of sickness in the camp.   → social
In case you think to send more pie, send two.
I'll try to bring you back some French perfume. distance

↳ sure of his return

When does a childhood end? Mothers
sew a piece of money inside a sock,
fathers unfold the map of the world, and boys
go off to war—that's an end, whether
they come back wrapped in the flag or waving it.
Sister and I were what they kissed goodbye,
complicitous in the long dream left behind.
On one page, willful innocence,
                                    on the next
an Army Captain writing from the ward
with few details and much regret—a kindness
she wouldn't forgive, and wouldn't be reconciled
to her soldier lost, or me in my luck, or the petals
strewn on the grass, or the boys still on the playground
routing evil with their little sticks.

To be brought from the bright schoolyard into the house:
to stand by her bed like an animal stunned in the pen:
against the grid of the quilt, her hand seems
stitched to the cuff of its sleeve—although he wants
most urgently the hand to stroke his head,
although he thinks he could kneel down
that it would need to travel only inches
to brush like a breath his flushed cheek,
he doesn't stir: all his resolve,
all his resources go to watching her,
her mouth, her hair a pillow of blackened ferns—
he means to match her stillness bone for bone.
Nearby he hears the younger children cry,
and his aunts, like careless thieves, out in the kitchen.

This is the double bed where she'd been born,
bed of her mother's marriage and decline,
bed her sisters also ripened in,
bed that drew her husband to her side,
bed of her one child lost and five delivered,
bed indifferent to the many bodies,
bed around which all of them were gathered,
watery shapes in the shadows of the room,
and the bed frail abroad the violent ocean,
the frightened beasts so clumsy and pathetic,
heaving their wet breath against her neck,
she threw off the pile of quilts—white face like a moon—
and then entered straightway into heaven.

anaphora: bed

The temperament of an artist but no art.
Papa got a piano just for her,
she used him best, made all the sisters try.
We rode the mule to lessons, birds on a branch—
you know what it meant to have your own piano?

Next, guitar. Then painting in pastels—
she stitched herself a smock, sketched a cow
she tied to the fence by the fringe of its tail, braided
the tail the cow left hanging there. Unschooled
in dance, too scornful of embroidery,

she seized on marriage like a lump of clay.
A husband is not clay. Unhappiness
I think can sap your health. Though by those lights
there's no good reason why I've lived this long.

When it was time to move, he didn't move,
he lay athwart his mother. She pushed and pushed—
she'd had a stone before, she wanted a child.

Reaching in, I turned him like a calf.
Rob gave her a piece of kindling wood,
she bit right through. I turned him twice.

Her sisters were all in the house, her brother
home again on leave—
                              in the months to come
in the cities there would be families
reported their terminals and fled,
                                            volunteers
would have to hunt the dying door-to-door.

It started here with too many breech and stillborn,
women who looked fifty not thirty-two.
I marked it childbed fever in my log.

Nothing would do but that he dig her grave,
under the willow oak, on high ground
beside the little graves, and in the rain—
a hard rain, and wind

enough to tear a limb from the limber tree.
His talk was wild, his eyes were polished stone,
all of him bent laboring to breathe—
even iron bends—

his face ash by the time he came inside.
Within the hour the awful cough began,
gurgling between coughs, and the fever spiked,
as his wife's had done.

Before a new day rinsed the windowpane,
he had swooned. Was blue.

a dear john letter

Dear Mattie, Pug says even a year of camp
would not help most of us so why not now.
Tomorrow we take a train to New York City,
board a freighter there. You know how the logs
are flushed through the long flume at Hodnetts' Mill,
the stream flooding the sluice, the cut pines
crowding and pushing and rushing, and then
the narrow chute opens onto the pond?
I'll feel like that, once we're out to sea
and seeing the world. I need to say
I've saved a bit, and you should also have
my Grandpa's watch—tell Fan that I said so.
Keep busy, pray for me, go on with Life,
and put your mind to a wedding in the yard—

less hopeful

In my sister's dream about the war
the animals had clearly human expressions
of grief and dread, maybe they were people
wearing animal bodies, cows at the fence,
hens in their nests. The older dog implored her
at the door; out back, aeroplanes
crossing overhead, she found the young one
motionless on the grass, open-eyed,
left leg bitten off, the meat and muscles
stripped back neatly from the jagged bone.
For weeks I thought that was my fiancé,
the mailbox was a shrine, I bargained with
the little god inside—I didn't know
it was us she saw in the bloody trenches.

My father's cousin Rawley in the Service,
we got word, and I think a neighbor's infant,
that was common, my mother'd lost one too.

Then he went to town to join the war.
The Sheriff hauled him home in an open rig:
spat on the street, been jailed a week or two.

She ran from the henhouse shrieking, shaking eggs
from the purse of her white apron to the ground.

Before I was born, he built a wide oak drainboard
in the kitchen, didn't just glue the boards,
screwed them down. Glue held, one split in two

My mother was an angel out of heaven.
My father was a viper. I wished him dead,
then he was dead. But she was too.

My brothers had it, my sister, parceled out
among the relatives, I had it exiled
in the attic room. Each afternoon
Grandfather came to the top stair, said
"How's my chickadee," and left me sweet
cream still in the crank. I couldn't eat it
but I hugged the sweaty bucket, I put
the chilled metal paddle against my tongue,
I swam in the quarry, into a nest of ropes,
they wrapped my chest, they kissed the soles of my feet
but not with kisses. Another time: a man
stooped in the open door with her packed valise,
my mother smoothing on eight-button gloves,
handing me a tooth, a sprig of rue—

O God, Thou hast cast us off, Thou hast scattered us,
Thou hast been displeased, O turn to us again.
Thou hast made the earth to tremble; Thou hast broken it;
heal the breaches thereof; for it shaketh.
Thou hast showed Thy people hard things; Thou hast made us
to drink the wine of astonishment.

Surely He shall deliver us from the snare,
He shall cover us with His feathers, and under His wings,
We shall not be afraid for the arrow by day
nor for the pestilence that walketh in darkness.
A thousand shall fall at our side, ten thousand shall fall,
but it shall not come nigh us, no evil befall us,
Because He hath set His love upon us. . . .

Here endeth the first lesson.

How can she be his mother—he had one of those
and knows she isn't it—odd, stiff,
negative of her sisters:
                like large
possessive animals they are, grooming
the small inscrutable faces with their spit.

But here's the boy, culled from the loud clump,
and she can give him courtesy and work,
and since he seems to love to play outside

they work his mother's garden, grubbing out
the weeds and grass, the marginal and frail,
staking the strongest fruit up from the dirt.

Together they'll put by what they don't eat,
jars and jars of it—greens, reds, yellows
blanched in the steaming kitchen, vats of brine.

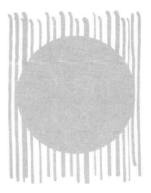

Hogs aren't pretty but they're smart,
and clean as you let them be—in a clean pen,
hogs are cleaner than your average cat:
they use their nose to push their shit aside.
And not lazy; if a hog
acts sick, you know it's sick.

As long as I've known hogs, I've known sick hogs,
especially in the fall, the cold and wet.
Before the weather goes, you slaughter hogs
unless you want to find them on their sides,
rheumy eyes, running snout.

It's simple enough arithmetic,
so don't you think the Kaiser knew?
Get one hog sick, you get them all.

more farm animals

Dear Mattie, Did you have the garden turned?
This morning early while I took my watch
I heard a wood sparrow—the song's the same
no matter what they call them over here—
remembered too when we were marching in,
the cottonwoods and sycamores and popples,
how fine they struck me coming from the ship
after so much empty flat gray sky,
on deck winds plowing up tremendous waves
and down below half the batallion ill.
Thirty-four we left behind in the sea
and more fell in the road, it's what took Pug.
But there's enough of us still and brave enough
to finish this quickly off and hurry home.

farm life

All day, one room: me, and the cherubim
with their wet kisses. Without quarantines,
who knew what was happening at home—
was someone put to bed, had someone died?
The paper said how dangerous, they coughed
and snuffed in their double desks, facing me—
they sneezed and spit on books we passed around
and on the boots I tied, retied, barely
out of school myself, Price at the front—
they smeared their lunch, they had no handkerchiefs,
no fresh water to wash my hands—when the youngest
started to cry, flushed and scared,
I just couldn't touch her, I let her cry.
Their teacher, and I let them cry.

Thought at first that grief had brought him down.
His wife dead, his own hand dug the grave
under a willow oak, in family ground—
he got home sick, was dead when morning came.

By week's end, his cousin who worked in town
was seized at once by fever and by chill,
left his office, walked back home at noon,
death ripening in him like a boil.

Soon it was a farmer in the field—
someone's brother, someone's father—
left the mule in its traces and went home.
Then the mason, the miller at his wheel,
from deep in the forest the hunter, the logger,
and the sun still up everywhere in the kingdom.

You wiped a fever-brow, you burned the cloth.
You scrubbed a sickroom floor, you burned the mop.
What wouldn't burn you boiled like applesauce
out beside the shed in the copper pot.
Apple, lightwood, linen, feather-bed—
it was the smell of that time, that neighborhood.
All night the pyre smouldered in the yard.
Your job: to obliterate what had been soiled.

But the bitten heart no longer cares for risk.
The orthodox still passed from lip to lip
the blessed relic and the ritual cup.
To see in the pile the delicate pillowslip
she'd worked by hand, roses and bluets—as if
hope could be fed by giving up—

religion

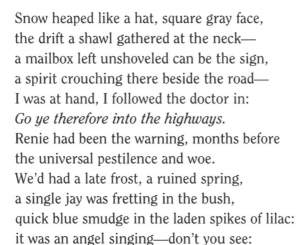

Snow heaped like a hat, square gray face,
the drift a shawl gathered at the neck—
a mailbox left unshoveled can be the sign,
a spirit crouching there beside the road—
I was at hand, I followed the doctor in:
Go ye therefore into the highways.
Renie had been the warning, months before
the universal pestilence and woe.
We'd had a late frost, a ruined spring,
a single jay was fretting in the bush,
quick blue smudge in the laden spikes of lilac:
it was an angel singing—don't you see:
it might as well have been a bush on fire.

A large lake, a little island in it.
Winter comes to the island and the ice
forms along the shore—when the first got sick
others came in to nurse them and it spread,
ice reaching out from the island into the lake.
Of course, there was another, larger shore—
Germany and Spain, New York, Atlanta,
ice also building *toward* the island.
By ice I'm thinking just those in the ground;
the sickness was more like brushfire in a clearing,
everyone beating the brush with coats and hands,
meanwhile the forest around us up in flames.
What was it like? I was small, I was sick,
I can't remember much—go study the graves.

spanish flu

Winter coming...
what does this
symbolize?

Circuit rider, magic leather credential at my feet
with its little vials of morphine and digitalis,
I made my rounds four days at a stretch
out from the village, in and out of their houses
and in between, in sunlight, moonlight,
nodding on the hard plank seat of the buggy—
it didn't matter which turn the old horse took:
illness flourished everywhere in the county.
At Foxes' the farmhouse doors were barred by snow;
they prised a board from a window to let me in.
At the next, one adult already dead,
the other too sick to haul the body out—

illness spreading

deep in the lungs a cloudiness not clearing;
vertigo, nausea, slowed heart, thick green catarrh,
nosebleeds spewing blood across the room—
as if it had conscripted all disease.
Once, finding a jug of homemade corn
beneath the bed where a whole fevered family
lay head to foot in their own and the others' filth,
I took a draught and split the rest among them,
even the children—these the very children named for me,
who had pulled them into this world—
it was the fourth day and my bag was empty,
small black bag I carried like a Bible.

—carried it everywhere

not looing ALL faith!

The barber, the teacher, the plumber, the preacher,
the man in a bowler, man in a cap,
the banker, the baker, the cabinet-maker,
the fireman, postman, clerk in the shop,

soldier and sailor, teamster and tailor,
man shoveling snow or sweeping his step,
carpenter, cobbler, liar, lawyer,
laid them down and never got up.

O, O, the world wouldn't stop—
the neighborhood grocer, the neighborhood cop
laid them down and never did rise.
And some of their children, and some of their wives,
fell into bed and never got up,
fell into bed and never got up.

bc of disease

set rhyme sheme
—childish sounding

Kyrie Eleison
—Lord have mercy

40

another letter

Dear Mattie, Though you don't tell of troubles there,
meaning to buy me peace I would suppose,
dreadful word goes around, families perished
or scattered. I remind myself Pug's mother
died from having him and he thought orphans
saved themselves some time in the scheme of things—
won't a future happiness be ransomed
by present woe? Dear Mattie, it's you
I think of when I say my prayers, your face,
it's you I'll want when I get back from this
just like the night that I said Marry me
and you said Yes, and the moon came
from behind the cloud as I had wished it to,
and I kissed your mouth, and then your chestnut hair.

angel of death

How we survived: we locked the doors
and let nobody in. Each night we sang.
Ate only bread in a bowl of buttermilk.
Boiled the drinking water from the well,
clipped our hair to the scalp, slept in steam.
Rubbed our chests with camphor, backs
with mustard, legs and thighs with fatback
and buried the rind. Since we had no lambs
I cut the cat's throat, Xed the door
and put the carcass out to draw the flies.
I raised an upstairs window and watched them go—
swollen, shiny, black, green-backed, green-eyed—
fleeing the house, taking the sickness with them.

Oh yes I used to pray. I prayed for the baby,
I prayed for my mortal soul as it contracted,
I prayed a gun would happen into my hand.
I prayed the way our nearest neighbors prayed,
head down, hands wrung, knees on the hard floor.
They all were sick and prayed to the Merciful Father
to send an angel, and my Henry came.
The least of these my brethren, Henry said.
Wherefore by my fruits, Henry said.
All of them survived—and do you think
they're still praying, thank you Lord for Henry?
She was so tiny, we kept her in a shoebox
on the cookstove, like a kitten.

What were they thinking—everyone we knew,
in school, in church, took me aside
to praise—to me—my sister, as if
I were another of her parents,
or else *they* were, that proud and fond:
aren't you lucky, isn't she gifted,
doesn't she look grand in her new blue suit?
I had a new suit cut from the same bolt,
quick mind, good heart—vivid blossoms
in other light—yes yes, she did, she was,
what were they thinking? Terrible,
to be the one who should have died.

Sweet are the songs of bitterness and blame,
against the stranger spitting on the street,
the neighbor's shared contaminated meal,
the rusted nail, the doctor come too late.

Sweet are the songs of envy and despair,
which count the healthy strangers that we meet
and mark the neighbors' illness mild and brief,
the birds that go on nesting, the brilliant air.

Sweet are the songs of wry exacted praise,
scraped from the grave, shaped in the torn throat
and sung at the helpful stranger on the train,
and at the neighbors misery brought near,
and at the waters parted at our feet,
and to the god who thought to keep us here.

He planned his own service, the pine box,
the open lid, which hymns, chapter and verse,
who would pray, how long, who'd carry him out.
He wrote it all down in a fair hand,
stroking the shawl around him in his chair,
and gave away his watch, his dog, his house.

Emmett said, he'd have lain down in the grave
except he needed us to tuck him in.

He shaved each day, put on his good wool pants
chosen for the cloth and a little loose
as they lowered in another son-in-law.
Sat by the door, handrolling cigarettes
three at a time, licking down both ends,
and wheezed and coughed and spit in a rusted can.

After I'd seen my children truly ill,
I had no need to dream that they were ill
nor in any other way imperiled—
no more babies pitching down the well,
no more watching from shore as my boy rolls
like a kicked stone from the raft, meanwhile
Kate with a handful of bees—
when I was a girl,
I practiced in the attic with my dolls,
but Del went out of right mind, his fingernails
turned blue, and Kate—no child should lie so still,
her small excitable body held enthralled. . . .
After that, in order to make it real
I dreamed them whole.

Dear Mat, For the red scarf I'm much obliged.
At first I couldn't wear it—bright colors
draw fire—but now I can. We took a shell
where three of us were washing out our socks
in a crater near my post. Good thing
the sock was off my foot since the foot's
all to pieces now—don't you fret,
it could have been my head, I've seen that here,
and then what use would be your pretty scarf?
The nurse bundles me up like an old man,
or a boy, and wheels me off the ward,
so many sick. But the Enemy suffers worse,
thanks to our gawdam guns as Pug would say.
Victory will come soon but without me.

The bride is in the parlor, dear confection.
Down on his knee at the edge of all that white,
her father puts a penny in her shoe.

Under the stiff organza and the sash,
the first cell of her first child slips
into the chamber with a little click.

The family next door was never struck
but we lost three—was that God's will? And which
were chosen for its purpose, us or them?

The Gospel says there is no us and them.
Science says there is no moral lesson.
The photo album says, who are these people?

After the paw withdraws, the world
hums again, making its golden honey.

Home a week, he woke thinking
he was back in France, under fire;
then thought the house on fire, the noise and light,
but that was from the fireworks and the torches
and on the square, a bonfire—everyone,
in nightclothes, emptied from their houses,
drawn toward a false dawn as from a cave—

oh there was dancing in the streets all right,
and singing—"Over There," "Yankee Doodle,"
"Mine Eyes Have Seen the Glory," I recall,
and "Camptown Races," who knows why—he plunged
into the crowd, tossed his crutch to the flames,
kissed delirious strangers on each side.

Say he lived through one war but not the other.

I told him not to move, they'd said *don't move.*
The weeks of fewer cases were a tease,

a winter thaw that froze back up worse
than before, backswing of a scythe, we filled

the gym, cots and pallets on the floor.
And many now in uniform—I could spot

who'd been gassed, their buttons were tarnished green—
and many of them were missing parts, like him.

Did I say the nurses were wearing masks?
My last day she put him next to me,

sweet little nurse but not enough of her
to go around she said *don't let him move.*

You tell me, was it prayer or luck kept
me from being that boy reaching for water?

I cried unto God with my voice . . . he gave ear unto me.
In the day of my trouble I sought the Lord;
   my sore ran in the night, and ceased not;
   my soul refused to be comforted.
I remembered God, and was troubled;
   I complained, and my spirit was overwhelmed.
I am so troubled I cannot speak.

Will the Lord cast off for ever? Is his mercy
   clean gone for ever? does his promise fail
   for evermore? Has God forgot to be gracious?
   has he in anger shut up his tender mercies?

Who is so great a God as our God?
   who has declared his strength among the people.

With no more coffins left, why not one wagon
plying all the shuttered neighborhoods,
calling for the dead, as they once did,
and let the living rest of us alone.
My father's pair of horses made the turn
at the big elm, onto the main road,
and we saw, strung out before us in the mud,
consecutive up the hill, links in a chain,
a caravan. Ahead of us in line:
three wrapped loaves. So I stared at the horse's head
between our mare's black ears, its brown ears framed
a gray, the gray a mule, until in the lead,
at the crest, was a child's toy, and a toy sled,
what lay in back shrunk to a cotterpin.

After they closed the schools the churches closed,
stacks like pulpwood filling the morgue,
but my cousin's husband's father "knew someone"
etcetera.
       Nobody else was there
but our own Parson Weems—to pray for us
and play the organ.
            Boy in a homemade box,
additional evergreens—rather grim
until the opening bars of "A Mighty Fortress"

flushed a bird from the pipes to agitate
around the nave. It's hard to cry if your head
is swiveled up,
         much less with bird manure
dropping "like the gentle rain"
on empty polished pews, plush carpet,
shut casket. Besides, I'd cried enough.

Who said the worst was past, who knew
such a thing? Someone writing history,
someone looking down on us
from the clouds. Down here, snow and wind:
cold blew through the clapboards,
our spring was frozen in the frozen ground.
Like the beasts in their holes,
no one stirred—if not sick
exhausted or afraid. In the village,
the doctor's own wife died in the night
of the nineteenth, 1919.
But it was true: at the window,
every afternoon, toward the horizon,
a little more light before the darkness fell.

Nothing fluttered, or sighed against her spine,
or coiled, recoiled in a fitful sleep,
fist in a sack, but her breasts knew
what her body made, and in her mind
she saw two legs, two arms, two plates of bone
where the damp tulle wings had been. Whatever it was,
she bled it out.

More snow fell,
into the deep ravine, the lesser gullies.
The doctor patted her arm: she was young, strong,
soon there would be another. But there wasn't:
just the one dream, the one scar.

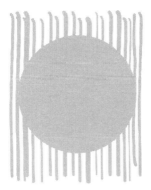

No longer just a stream, not yet a pond,
the water slowed and deepened, banks eroded,
redwing blackbird roosting on a stalk,
sometimes that rippled vee plowing the surface.
Each clear day, she walked to the willow oak,
raked the anemic grass, tidied the mounds,
walked back down to the house by way of the creek.
If the beaver had put in a stick, she took it out.
If a storm had dropped a branch, she hauled it off.
When milder weather came, she tucked her skirts
at the waist and waded in, dislodging trash
the beaver would recover. Months of this.
Twice she sent for the neighbor to trap it or shoot it,
but each time Fan said Emmett don't you dare.

Once the world had had its fill of war,
in a secret wood, as the countryside lay stunned,
at the hour of the wolf and the vole, in a railroad car,
the generals met and put their weapons down.
Like spring it was, as word passed over all
the pocked and riven ground, and underground;
now the nations sat in a gilded hall,
dividing what they'd keep of what they'd won.

And so the armies could be done with war,
and soldiers trickled home to study peace.
But the old gardens grew a tough new weed,
and the old lives didn't fit as they had before,
and where there'd been the dream, a stranger's face,
and where there'd been the war, an empty sleeve.

To claim the War alone changed everything
can't be entirely right, too few of us
went over there.
  My mother used to phone—
the telephone was new, electric lights,
cars among the horses on the street—
my mother every morning when we woke
rang around to see who else had died.
She and Uncle Henry had a faith
deaf as well as blind, but most of us,
the orphans and the watchers and the stung—

at recess there was a favorite game: the chosen
died, in fits and twitches, while the other
stood by to cross the arms on the chest—that angels
might get a better grip—and to weep.

Maybe the soul *is* breath. The door shut,
the doctor, needed elsewhere, on his rounds,
the bereaved withdrawn, preoccupied with grief,
I pack each orifice with hemp, or gauze,
arrange the limbs, wash the flesh—at least
a last brief human attention,
                                                not like
those weeks the train brought in big wicker
baskets we had to empty and return,
bodies often so blue we couldn't tell
who was Colored, who was White, which
holy or civil ground to send them to,
plots laid out by dates instead of names. . . .

Have you ever heard a dead man sigh?
A privilege, that conversation.

Around the house uneasy stillness falls.
The dog stiffens the ruff at her ears,
stands, looks to the backdoor, looks to the stairwell,
licks her master's shoe. What she hears

must be a pitch high on the Orphic scale,
a light disturbance in the air,
like flicks of an insect's wings or a reed's whistle
distant and brief: he barely stirs.

Out in the kitchen something seems to settle—
cloth on a dish, dust on a chair?
The animal whimpers now but doesn't growl:
this absence has a smell.
                         Poor master,
it's touched him too, that shift in molecules,
but all he feels is more of what's not there.

I had other children, and they've all
had children too, I know I am
the luckiest of men—my wife, my sons—
but the tongue goes to where the tooth had been.

He was our first. The War, he said,
was the one important story of his time,
a crucible.
            Right after he got sick
they quarantined the post, we were on our way
to nurse him through—
                      our brightest boy
who used to ride his horse the length of the trestle,
across the steep ravine of Cherrystone,
he had such faith in the horse, in himself—

we stayed at a little inn, they gave us Tea,
served the English way, with clotted cream.

I always thought she ought to have an angel.
There's one I saw a picture of, smooth white,
the wings like bolts of silk, breasts like a girl's—
like hers—eyebrows, all of it. For years
I put away a little every year,
but her family was shamed by the bare grave,
and hadn't they blamed me for everything,
so now she has a cross. Crude, rigid, nothing
human in it, flat dead tree on the hill,
it's what you see for miles, it's all I see.
Symbol of hope, the priest said, clearing his throat,
and the rain came down and washed the formal flowers.
I guess he thinks that dusk is just like dawn.
I guess he had forgot about the nails.

If doubts have wintered over in your house,
they won't go out. The residue in the cupboard
means they've built a nest of your neglect
and fattened in it, and multiply, like mice.
Soft gray velvet scurry on the floor?
The rational cat licks a foot and looks away.
All dread passes—any harm they do
is mostly out of sight, and it's not just
your failure anyway:
                        a plausible God
is a God of rapture, if not the falcon
at least the small decorous ribbon snake
that slept in the hay against the northern wall.
But look: what drips like a limp Chinese moustache
at the lips of the cat coming up the cellarstairs?

My mother died, I was eight, I was sent away—
that has no meaning, just a shape,
the room I've lived in. That morning, end of May,

there'd been a frost so hard it looked like snow,
white on the green fields, the startled cows.
Spring in the fields, wild onion spikes the clover—

so bitter, even the butter ruined.
I've known some to dump it at the barn,
but if I bought a lamp that didn't burn

I wouldn't dump the oil, I'd soak the wick.
Eating a slice raw will do the work:
you notice nothing in the milk but milk.

He stands by the bed, he sits beside the bed,
he lays his unfledged body on the bed
where she had lain. If he'd had the right words
in his prayer, if he'd stayed awake
all night, if he'd been good, been wise, perhaps
he could have brought her back, the way she drew him
out of his dark moods, guitar in her lap,
her hair lace and shadow on her cheek—
in the hard-backed book propped open by the lamp
the shape-notes swarmed like minnows on the page,
she'd said their lives were scripted there.
Nearby someone feeds the treasonous baby.
She lied is the first verse of his new life.

To have inherited a child, angry
and grieving; to have opened her rusted heart
that first full inch; to feel it seize on the cold air
rushing in; and now to pretend his story,
lost in the deep thicket of the others,
is not hers: he stole again from the store,
she whipped him home and locked him in the barn,
he set the barn on fire and ran away.
How could that be her sister's boy, asleep
in the trundle bed, or ratcheting through the field—
he loved to be outside—from the porch she'd see
the top of his head, golden as the wheat,
parting the wheat, and then the wheat
closing up behind him without a seam.

Girls adore their teacher in third grade,
boys wait till they're grown. They send a card,
they visit now and again, wives in the car,
and I squint to find in the formed face
the face I knew, that little ghost. Time
isn't a straight line, it's a scummy pond
our minds fish in, and I might hook
Price alive instead of me
but not the two of us, in the dream we'd had—
that's been crowded out by the actual,
my husband, those borrowed children. After lunch
it's Once Upon a Time—my gift to them—
always the same few stories, can't change a word,
it eases them to know how they will end.

What I remember best is my cousin's crow.
He found it, fed it, splinted its damaged wing,
and it came when he whistled it down, ate from his hand,
said, like a slow child, what he had said.
Emmett never used a leash or cage;
for a year it hulked in the big pine by the door
or in the windmill's metal scaffold, descending
for apple, a little grain, a little show.

Once God gave out free will, I bet He was sorry.
So much had been invested in the bird,
the bird not understanding gratitude.
Well again, it turned up in the yard
from time to time, no longer smart or amusing,
no longer *his,* just another crow.

Dear Mattie, Wanting this right I'll write it down.
At the rally, I signed up for the War.
My father wanted that, and Fan was there
with Del and Kate and A. T. Cocke, Rob
and Renie and their children waving flags,
the Hodnetts and the Foxes next to them,
Dr. Gilmore Reynolds on his porch,
and Rawley a hero in his uniform.
Your uncle held the Bible for the oath,
everyone cheered—could you and your sister hear it
down at the school? It was the best birthday,
are you proud of me, we hadn't thought
to be married anyway before the fall,
I should be home to bring the harvest in

Why did you have to go back, go back
to that awful time, upstream, scavenging
the human wreckage, what happened or what we did
or failed to do? Why drag us back to the ditch?
Have you no regard for oblivion?

History is organic, a great tree,
along the starched corduroy of its bark
the healed scars, the seasonal losses
so asymmetrical, so common—
why should you set out to count?

Don't you people have sufficient woe?

EPILOGUE

The snow against the glass is full of sleet,
loud sheets of it, lined on a strict diagonal,
a scrim between the farmhouse and the hill.

Marking the blurred horizon, five stiff trees,
windbreak—the residue as woods were pared away—
extended east and west by stone walls made

from what the earth cast up and didn't need.
Summer, under dumb clouds still benign, maternal,
as the narrow local stream rushed toward salt,

the drayhorse grazed where open field had been,
kneedeep in thistles, milkweed, fireweed, Queen Anne's lace,
his back a sprung hammock withers to tail,

his gut slung low and parallel, his sex,
unloosed from its suede holster, dimpled as crepe. Now
every stalk in the field is beaten down.

Such is the world our world is nestled in.
And what if the horse were installed in the barn with a bucket
    of oats?
Shush, says winter, blown against the window.

AUTHOR'S NOTE

In March 1918, what the Germans would call "Flanders Fever" was first recorded at Camp Funston, Kansas; in April, disabled ninety recruits a day at Fort Devins; in May, struck 90 percent of the American forces at Dunkirk; by June, had infected eight million Spaniards; July, spread widely throughout India; August, sprouted in China and returned to New York on board a Norwegian ship; September, reached eighty-five thousand civilian cases in Massachusetts alone; on one October day, claimed seven hundred recorded deaths in Philadelphia; in November, subsided long enough for the repeal of laws that forbade shaking hands (Arizona) or required masks on public transport (San Francisco); then reemerged, more virulent and often among the same populations, as the troops came home. By March 1919, "Spanish" influenza had killed, by conservative estimate, more than twenty-five million worldwide.

Most of the victims were neither old nor very young nor particularly frail: the virus favored young adults, and the normal *U* curve of mortality figures warped into a Dutch girl's pointed hat. Once past the usual childhood diseases, the body redeploys its defenses against more localized dangers, such as broken bones or wounds, for which the best response is inflammation: flooding the site with antibodies, white cells. This time, the infection was generalized—the entire interior surface of the lungs. On autopsy, normally delicate lung tissue was dense and sodden, the lungs two blue sacks of fluid. The victims drowned.

The U.S. toll was half a million dead: as many servicemen killed by influenza as in combat, and ten times that many civilians. The figure does not include stillborns and women lost in childbirth, numbers elevated in the early months, nor the increase in deaths from pneumonia and tuberculosis during the epidemic period, nor those in whom the virus exacerbated a previous condition such as heart disease or pleurisy.

In one year, one quarter of the total U.S. population contracted influenza; one out of five never recovered. Nevertheless, the national memory bears little trace. There are few notable records in our imaginative literature: Katherine Anne Porter's *Pale Horse, Pale Rider;* Willa Cather's *One of Ours;* Horton Foote's *Home Cycle;* and William Maxwell's *They Came Like Swallows.* A well-researched account is available from Alfred W. Crosby, *America's Forgotten Pandemic: The Influenza of 1918* (Cambridge University Press, 1989), from which the statistics cited here have been taken.

ACKNOWLEDGMENTS

The poems beginning "Nothing fluttered or sighed against her spine" and "I always thought she ought to have an angel" appeared juxtaposed to specific artworks in collections published by The University of Iowa Press and the Chicago Art Institute, respectively. The last Mattie poem, "Girls adore their teacher . . . ," is dedicated to Marge Sable.

I would also like to recognize here the immensely valuable responses of my early readers, and to thank in particular Carol Houck Smith for her encouragement in this project.